The Battle of the Alamo

Kerri O'Hern
AR B.L.: 4.2
Points: 0.5                    MG

# GRAPHIC HISTORIES
# THE BATTLE OF THE ALAMO

**STORY:**
KERRI O'HERN AND JANET RIEHECKY

**ILLUSTRATIONS:**
D. MCHARGUE

WORLD ALMANAC® LIBRARY

# REMEMBER THE ALAMO!

IN 1836, TEXAS BELONGED TO MEXICO. BUT MOST TEXANS WANTED THEIR OWN GOVERNMENT. ON MARCH 6, 200 TEXANS BATTLED 2,000 MEXICAN SOLDIERS AT THE ALAMO IN TEXAS. THE TEXANS FOUGHT FOR THEIR INDEPENDENCE.

AMERICANS TODAY REMEMBER THE BATTLE AT THE ALAMO AS A FIGHT FOR FREEDOM.

LONG BEFORE THE TEXANS AND MEXICANS FOUGHT AT THE ALAMO, NATIVE PEOPLES LIVED IN TEXAS. THE CADDO INDIANS BUILT VILLAGES, HUNTED ANIMALS, AND RAISED CROPS IN THE AREA.

THE CADDO CALLED THEMSELVES TEJAS, MEANING "FRIEND." THIS WORD GRADUALLY BECAME THE NAME FOR THE WHOLE AREA. LATER, ENGLISH SPEAKERS CHANGED IT TO "TEXAS."

EXPLORERS FROM SPAIN MET THE CADDO IN THE 1500s. THE SPANISH EXPLORERS CAME TO LOOK FOR GOLD. THEY DECIDED TO STAY AND TAKE CONTROL OF THIS LAND.

IN 1682, SEVERAL CATHOLIC PRIESTS FROM SPAIN BUILT A MISSION IN TEXAS. A MISSION IS A PLACE WHERE RELIGION IS TAUGHT. THE PRIESTS TAUGHT THE NATIVE PEOPLE ABOUT CHRISTIANITY.

BONG

THE SPANISH BUILT SEVERAL MISSIONS OVER THE NEXT FEW DECADES. ONE WAS BUILT NEAR THE SAN ANTONIO RIVER. THIS MISSION GREW IN SIZE UNTIL IT HAD SEVERAL BUILDINGS AND A COURTYARD. WALLS SURROUNDED THE BUILDING, AND WATER FLOWED THROUGH THE MIDDLE.

MOST NATIVE PEOPLES DID NOT WANT TO CHANGE THEIR RELIGION, SO THE MISSION CLOSED. IN 1801, THE SPANISH BEGAN USING THESE BUILDINGS AS A MILITARY FORT. THE SOLDIERS NAMED THIS FORT "THE ALAMO."

ACROSS THE RIVER FROM THE ALAMO, THE TOWN OF SAN ANTONIO DE BÉXAR GREW. PEOPLE MOVED INTO TOWN AND STORES SPRANG UP.

VIVA MÉXICO!

THE SPANISH HAD BEEN RULING MEXICO SINCE THE MID 1500s. THE SPANISH HAD THE WEALTH AND POWER, WHILE MOST OF THE MEXICAN INDIANS LIVED IN POVERTY. AFTER 10 YEARS OF FIGHTING, THE MEXICANS WON THEIR FREEDOM IN 1821.

MEXICO BECAME AN INDEPENDENT NATION, AND TEXAS BECAME A PROVINCE RULED BY MEXICO. FOR A FEW YEARS, THE MEXICAN CITIZENS HELPED DECIDE THE LAWS OF MEXICO.

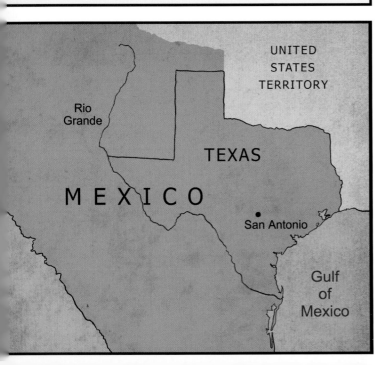

UNITED STATES TERRITORY

Rio Grande

TEXAS

M E X I C O

San Antonio

Gulf of Mexico

BUT IN 1833, GENERAL ANTONIO LÓPEZ DE SANTA ANNA DECLARED HIMSELF PRESIDENT OF MEXICO. SOON HE MADE ALL THE LAWS.

MEXICO'S NEW GOVERNMENT WANTED PEOPLE TO SETTLE THE LAND IN TEXAS. DURING THE 1820s, WHITE AMERICAN, OR ANGLO, FAMILIES BEGAN MOVING THERE.

LAND WAS CHEAP, SO MANY SET UP LARGE RANCHES. SOME ANGLOS BROUGHT SLAVES TO WORK THE LAND. THE MEXICANS DID NOT PAY MUCH ATTENTION TO TEXAS. THE ANGLOS THERE MADE THEIR OWN RULES.

BY THE MID 1830s, ANGLOS MADE UP THREE-FOURTHS OF THE TOTAL POPULATION IN TEXAS. THESE ANGLOS IGNORED SANTA ANNA'S LAWS. THEY SMUGGLED, HAD SLAVES, AND DID NOT PAY TAXES.

ATTENTION
NO ANGLO SETTLERS
MAY ENTER
MEXICAN
TERRITORIES
BY ORDER OF THE MEXICAN GOVERNMENT ORDER 65-TH

ATTENTION
NO ANGLO SETTLERS
MAY ENTER MEXICAN TERRITORIES
BY ORDER OF THE MEXICAN GOVERNMENT ORDER 65-TH

NO MORE AMERICAN SETTLERS WERE ALLOWED TO MOVE INTO TEXAS. MEXICAN SOLDIERS MOVED TO TEXAS TO ENFORCE MEXICAN LAWS.

THE ANGLO SETTLERS STILL HAD AMERICAN IDEAS. THEY BELIEVED CITIZENS SHOULD HAVE A SAY IN THEIR GOVERNMENT. WHEN SANTA ANNA BECAME PRESIDENT, HE TOOK AWAY MANY RIGHTS AND INCREASED HIS OWN POWERS.

THE SETTLERS WERE DIVIDED ABOUT HOW TO HANDLE THEIR ANGER TOWARD SANTA ANNA. SOME WANTED TO REMAIN LOYAL TO MEXICO—THEY WERE CALLED THE "PEACE PARTY." OTHERS WANTED INDEPENDENCE FROM MEXICO—THEY WERE CALLED THE "WAR PARTY."

WILLIAM TRAVIS, A LAWYER FROM SOUTH CAROLINA, JOINED THE WAR PARTY IN 1831.

IN JUNE 1835, A GROUP OF 25 MEN LED BY WILLIAM TRAVIS ATTACKED A MEXICAN FORT AT ANAHUÁC.

LONG LIVE TEXAS!

ARMED WITH ONLY A CANNON, THEY DEMANDED THAT THE MEXICANS GIVE UP THE FORT.

DON'T COME BACK!

THEY GOT IT WITHOUT A FIGHT.

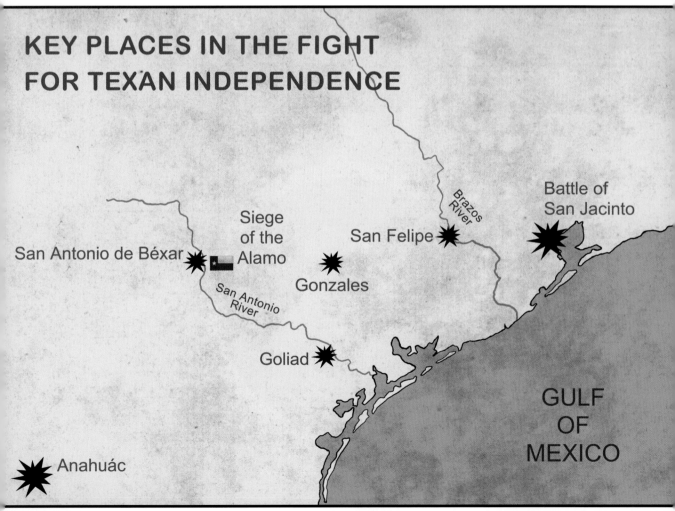

# KEY PLACES IN THE FIGHT FOR TEXAN INDEPENDENCE

Brazos River

Battle of San Jacinto

Siege of the Alamo

San Felipe

San Antonio de Béxar

San Antonio River

Gonzales

Goliad

GULF OF MEXICO

Anahuác

AFTER THE FIGHT AT GONZALES, AMERICAN VOLUNTEERS POURED INTO TEXAS TO FIGHT. THESE VOLUNTEERS WERE NOT REGULAR SOLDIERS, BUT MANY WERE EXCELLENT HUNTERS AND RIFLEMEN.

NEXT!

GENERAL AUSTIN OF THE REBEL ARMY LED AN ATTACK ON THE MEXICAN HEADQUARTERS AT BÉXAR. WITH THE HELP OF 500 VOLUNTEERS, THE TEXANS SURROUNDED THE ALAMO.

**MEANWHILE...**

IT'S TIME FOR A REVOLUTION!

IN NOVEMBER 1835, A GROUP OF 57 TEXANS MET IN SAN FELIPE AND WROTE "A DECLARATION OF CAUSES." THIS DOCUMENT LISTED THE REASONS THAT TEXANS SHOULD REBEL AGAINST MEXICO. THE ANGLOS IN TEXAS SET UP THEIR OWN GOVERNMENT, ELECTING HENRY SMITH AS GOVERNOR. SAM HOUSTON BECAME COMMANDER OF THE REBEL ARMY.

UNANIMOUS
DECLARATION OF INDEPENDENCE,
BY THE
DELEGATES OF THE PEOPLE OF TEXAS,
IN GENERAL CONVENTION,
AT THE TOWN OF WASHINGTON,

General Austin

Commander Houston

YOU WILL GO BACK!

YES SIR

AND YOU WILL TAKE BACK THE ALAMO!

SANTA ANNA WAS VERY ANGRY. HE SENT A LARGE ARMY TO TAKE BACK BÉXAR AND THE ALAMO.

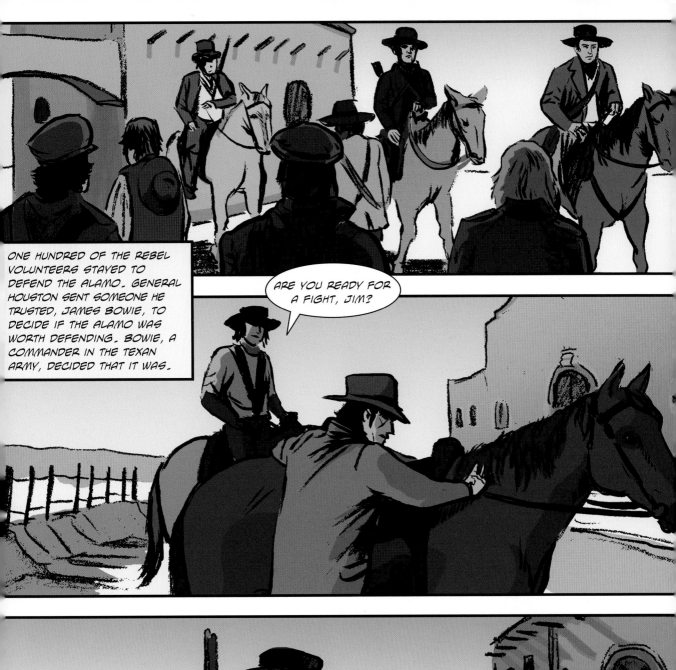

ONE HUNDRED OF THE REBEL VOLUNTEERS STAYED TO DEFEND THE ALAMO. GENERAL HOUSTON SENT SOMEONE HE TRUSTED, JAMES BOWIE, TO DECIDE IF THE ALAMO WAS WORTH DEFENDING. BOWIE, A COMMANDER IN THE TEXAN ARMY, DECIDED THAT IT WAS.

ARE YOU READY FOR A FIGHT, JIM?

GOVERNOR SMITH SENT WILLIAM TRAVIS, A LIEUTENANT COLONEL IN THE TEXAN ARMY, TO HELP DEFEND THE ALAMO.

BOWIE AND TRAVIS EACH HAD ARRIVED WITH 30 MEN. THEN, 12 SHARPSHOOTERS LED BY DAVY CROCKETT ARRIVED. OTHER HUNTERS AND FUR TRAPPERS CAME TO JOIN IN THE FIGHT TOO. STILL, THE ALAMO HAD ONLY A FEW HUNDRED DEFENDERS.

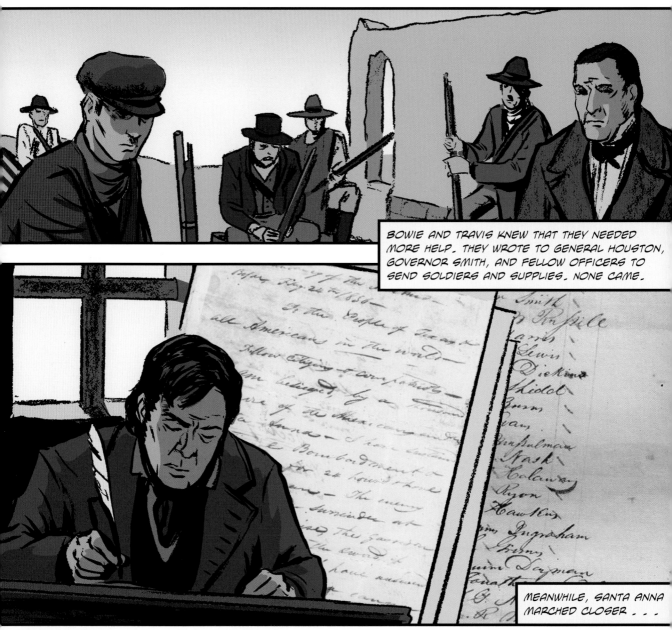

BOWIE AND TRAVIS KNEW THAT THEY NEEDED MORE HELP. THEY WROTE TO GENERAL HOUSTON, GOVERNOR SMITH, AND FELLOW OFFICERS TO SEND SOLDIERS AND SUPPLIES. NONE CAME.

MEANWHILE, SANTA ANNA MARCHED CLOSER . . .

SANTA ANNA AND HIS ARMY ARRIVED ON FEBRUARY 23, 1836.

GET INSIDE!

IMMEDIATELY, EVERYONE NEARBY RETREATED BEHIND THE ALAMO'S WALLS, QUICKLY GRABBING FOOD AND SUPPLIES.

SANTA ANNA RAISED A RED FLAG WITH SKULL AND CROSSBONES. THE FIGHT WAS ON!

HIS MEN SURROUNDED THE ALAMO AND FIRED CANNONS AT THE WALLS.

OVER AND OVER FOR 13 DAYS, THE CANNONBALLS HIT THE ALAMO.

INSIDE THE ALAMO, SUPPLIES RAN LOW. THE TEXANS FELT HUNGRY, THIRSTY, AND COLD. SEVERAL VOLUNTEERS SNUCK OUT TO GET MORE FOOD, WATER, AND FIREWOOD.

IN ADDITION, ABOUT 30 MORE VOLUNTEERS ACTUALLY SNUCK INTO THE ALAMO. THEY WANTED TO HELP FIGHT.

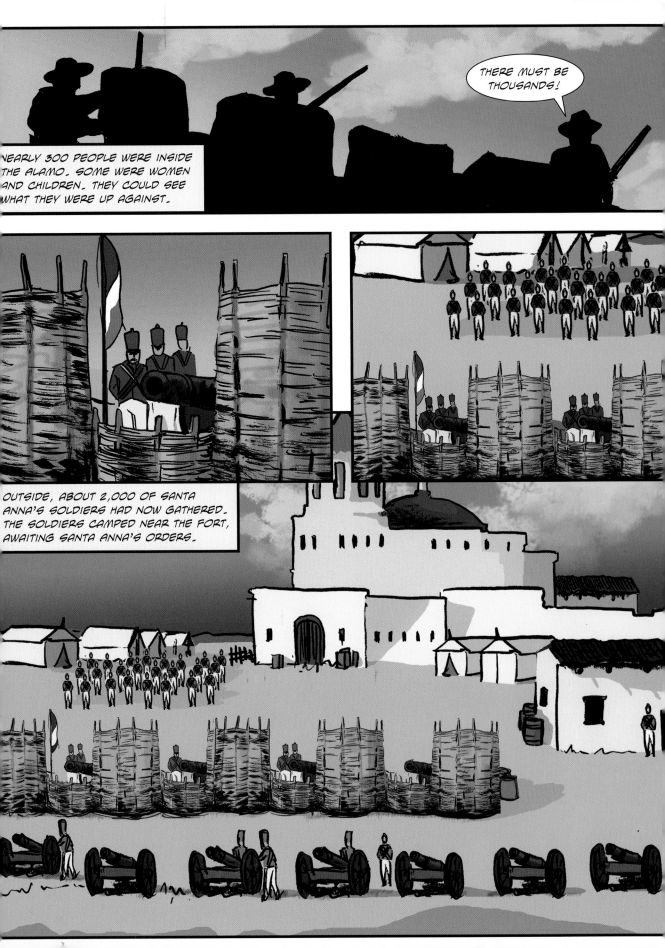

THERE MUST BE THOUSANDS!

NEARLY 300 PEOPLE WERE INSIDE THE ALAMO. SOME WERE WOMEN AND CHILDREN. THEY COULD SEE WHAT THEY WERE UP AGAINST.

OUTSIDE, ABOUT 2,000 OF SANTA ANNA'S SOLDIERS HAD NOW GATHERED. THE SOLDIERS CAMPED NEAR THE FORT, AWAITING SANTA ANNA'S ORDERS.

AFTER MIDNIGHT ON MARCH 6, 1836, THE ORDERS CAME.

SANTA ANNA TOLD HIS SOLDIERS TO REMOVE THEIR COATS AND BLANKETS. HE DID NOT WANT THEM TO TRIP OR MAKE NOISE WHILE THEY MOVED. SANTA ANNA ORDERED THEM TO TAKE POSITIONS AROUND THE ALAMO AND PREPARE FOR A FULL ATTACK.

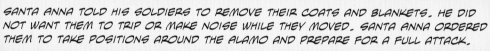

JUST BEFORE DAWN, THE ATTACK BEGAN.

ATTACK!

VIVA MÉXICO!

THE TEXANS WERE SURPRISED BY THE ATTACK. WORN OUT BY DAYS WITHOUT SLEEP, MANY WERE SICK.

MAKE EVERY BULLET COUNT, BOYS!

STILL, THEY FOUND THEIR POSITIONS. SOON THE FOUR WALLS INSIDE THE ALAMO WERE LINED WITH TEXAN SHARPSHOOTERS.

THE FIRST GROUP OF MEXICAN SOLDIERS NEVER MADE IT TO THE ALAMO'S WALLS. TEXAN SHARPSHOOTERS KILLED THOSE SOLDIERS.

BUT WAVE AFTER WAVE OF MEXICAN SOLDIERS CONTINUED TO COME.

UGH!

THE MEXICANS FIRED CANNONS INTO THE ALAMO. ONE OF THE FIRST SHOTS HIT TRAVIS IN THE HEAD AND KILLED HIM.

AS THE TEXANS HELD THEIR POSITIONS IN THE ALAMO, THE MEXICANS CHARGED FORWARD AGAIN. THIS TIME THEY HAD A BETTER PLAN.

POW

LOOK SHARP!

MEXICAN SOLDIERS BELOW TOOK AIM AT THE SHARPSHOOTERS WHILE . . .

. . . OTHERS THREW LADDERS AGAINST THE NORTH WALL.

THEY'RE EVERYWHERE!

UP, UP, UP THE SOLDIERS SWARMED, FACING GUNFIRE AT EVERY STEP.

SHOOT!

AT LAST, THEY REACHED THE TOP!

WITHIN A FEW HOURS, MEXICAN SOLDIERS FILLED THE INSIDE OF THE ALAMO.

CHARGE!

POW

THEY SEIZED CONTROL OF THE WALLS AND FIRED ON THE TEXANS WITHIN.

THE TEXANS CONTINUED TO FIGHT.

THEY'RE INSIDE!

BUT THEY WERE VASTLY OUTNUMBERED.

FALL BACK!

PEOPLE RAN IN EVERY DIRECTION! MOST OF THE TEXANS DIED QUICKLY.

TO THE CHURCH!

SEVERAL HID IN THE CHURCH AND THE BUILDINGS ALONG THE EAST WALL.

THE TEXANS USED ANY WEAPON THEY COULD. WITH EMPTY RIFLES, THEY BEAT AT THE MEXICANS. TOMAHAWKS AND KNIVES FLASHED OUT. BUT NEARLY ALL THE TEXANS WERE KILLED.

A FEW TEXANS TRIED TO SURRENDER, BUT THE MEXICANS SHOT THEM.

POOM

SOMETIME BETWEEN 6:00 AND 9:30 A.M. THE BATTLE WAS OVER.

ONLY A FEW TEXANS SURVIVED.

ABOUT 500 MEXICAN SOLDIERS HAD DIED.

TEXANS WANTED TO GET REVENGE FOR THEIR LOSS AT THE ALAMO. ON APRIL 21, 1836, GENERAL HOUSTON LED HIS ARMY IN AN ATTACK AGAINST THE MEXICAN ARMY ON THE SAN JACINTO PLAINS. THE MEXICAN TROOPS WERE CAUGHT OFF GUARD. COLONEL SIDNEY SHERMAN OF THE TEXAN ARMY SHOUTED, "REMEMBER THE ALAMO!" THE BATTLE LASTED ONLY EIGHTEEN MINUTES. THE TEXANS WON. THE VERY NEXT DAY, THE TEXANS CAPTURED SANTA ANNA.

William Travis

Davy Crockett

Jim Bowie

HOUSTON GOT SANTA ANNA TO GRANT INDEPENDENCE TO TEXAS. IN SEPTEMBER 1836, HOUSTON WAS ELECTED PRESIDENT OF THE NEW REPUBLIC OF TEXAS. IN 1845, TEXAS BECAME THE TWENTY-EIGHTH U.S. STATE.

THE TEXANS WHO DEFENDED THE ALAMO ARE A SYMBOL OF COURAGE. THEY WERE OUTNUMBERED, BUT STILL THEY FOUGHT. "REMEMBER THE ALAMO" ECHOES DOWN THROUGH U.S. HISTORY. IT STANDS FOR COURAGE AGAINST IMPOSSIBLE ODDS.

# MORE BOOKS TO READ

*The Alamo.* Ann Gaines (Child's World)

*The Alamo in American History.* Roy Sorrels (Enslow Publishers)

*The Battle of the Alamo: The Fight for Texas Territory.* Carmen Bredeson (Lerner Publishing Group)

*Inside the Alamo.* Jim Murphy (Bantum Doubleday Dell Books for Young Readers)

*The Siege of the Alamo.* Landmark Events in American History (series). Janet Riehecky. (World Almanac Library)

# WEB SITES

*Alamo History from The Daughters of the Republic of Texas Library*
www.drtl.org/History/index.asp

*The Alamo Site*
www.thealamofilm.com

*Remember the Alamo*
www.pbs.org/wgbh/amex/alamo/peopleevents/e_alamo.html

*Texas Almanac*
www.texasalmanac.com/history/highlights/alamo/

*The Handbook of Texas Online*
www.tsha.utexas.edu/handbook/online/articles/AA/qea2.html

Please visit our web site at: www.worldalmanaclibrary.com
For a free color catalog describing World Almanac® Library's list of high-quality books and multimedia programs, call 1-800-848-2928 (USA) or 1-800-387-3178 (Canada). World Almanac® Library's fax: (414) 332-3567.

**Library of Congress Cataloging-in-Publication Data**

O'Hern, Kerri.
 The battle of the Alamo / Kerri O'Hern and Janet Riehecky.
 p. cm. — (Graphic histories)
 Includes bibliographical references.
 ISBN 0-8368-6201-5 (lib. bdg.)
 ISBN 0-8368-6253-8 (softcover)
 1. Alamo (San Antonio, Tex.)—Juvenile literature. 2. Alamo (San Antonio, Tex.)—Siege, 1836—Juvenile literature. 3. Texas—History—To 1846—Juvenile literature. 4. San Antonio (Tex.)--Buildings, structures, etc.--Juvenile literature. I. Riehecky, Janet, 1953- II. Title. III. Series.
 F390.O38 2006
 976.4'03—dc22                                  2005027870

First published in 2006 by
**World Almanac® Library**
A Member of the WRC Media Family of Companies
330 West Olive Street, Suite 100
Milwaukee, WI 53212 USA

Copyright © 2006 by World Almanac® Library.

Produced by Design Press, a division of the
Savannah College of Art and Design
Design: Janice Shay and Maria Angela Rojas
Editing: Kerri O'Hern
Illustration: D. McHargue
World Almanac® Library editorial direction: Mark Sachner
 and Valerie J. Weber
World Almanac® Library art direction: Tammy West

Printed in the United States of America

1 2 3 4 5 6 7 8 9 10 09 08 07 06